The Linguistics of Light

Lisa Dart was born in Cornwall, but grew up in Orpington, Kent in England. After working for both the Open University and the University of Sussex for many years, she combines writing poetry with her commitment to gifted children as Head of Curriculum Enhancement at St Bede's School. Her chapbook was published by Tall Lighthouse in 2005 and she was one of the four winners for the USA Grolier Prize 2004. Many of her poems have appeared in British poetry magazines. She has recently completed a doctorate in poetry and philosophy at the University of Sussex.

The Linguistics of Light

LISA DART

CAMBRIDGE

PUBLISHED BY SALT PUBLISHING
14a High Street, Fulbourn, Cambridge CB21 5DH United Kingdom

© Lisa Dart, 2009

The right of Lisa Dart to be identified as the
author of this work has been asserted by her in accordance
with Section 77 of the Copyright, Designs and Patents Act 1988.

Salt Publishing 2009

Printed and bound in the United Kingdom by MPG Books Group

Typeset in Swift 9.5 / 13

ISBN 978 1 84471 445 2 hardback

Salt Publishing Ltd gratefully acknowledges
the financial assistance of Arts Council England

1 3 5 7 9 8 6 4 2

for L

Contents

Acknowledgements

I would like to thank all my fellow D. Phil students for the wonderful day schools: the advice, questions and comments as well as the humour shared on those days added much to my understanding of writing and revising poems. I would also like to thank Andrea Hollander Budy, Alistair Davies, Tobias Hill, Andie Lewenstein and Paul Matthews for their sensitive comments on early versions of many of these poems.

Thank you is too small a word for my partner for all his encouragement and love.

Some of the poems have been accepted for publication in the following poetry journals: *Agenda*, *Caduceus*, *Envoi*, *Orbis*, *Scintilla*, *Succour*, *Tears in the Fence*, *The Interpreter's House*, *The New Writer*.

'The Word' and 'Held' were published in the anthology *Into the Further Reaches*. 'Garra Rock' was published in the eco-anthology *Earth Songs*.

'Couples' and 'Arkansas in March' were published as one of four winners for the *Grolier Poetry Prize* in America, 2004.

In 2005 Tall Lighthouse published twelve poems in a pamphlet entitled *The Self in the Photograph*.

'The Failing Light' was published in *Automatic lighthouse: the second tall-lighthouse poetry review*, 2006

'Derek Jarman's Garden' and an earlier version of 'Winter in Hampden Park' were published in *City lighthouse: the third tall-lighthouse poetry review*, 2009.

Only where there is language is there a world. Without the retaining word, the whole of things, the 'world' sinks into darkness, together with the 'I'. . .

Derek Jarman's Garden, Dungeness

Busy old fool, unruly sun,
Why dost thou thus
Through windows and through curtains call on us?
　　　　　　　　　　　　　— JOHN DONNE

We drive through a burnt October,
trees turning, sun in almost mist.
You give directions, more from the landscape
than our atlas *where*, you said, *nothing*
that really gives us bearing exists.

Prospect Cottage— stones set
in a scarcity of green, driftwood stumps
framed by concrete waste.
A wind lifts without reverence
remnants of rusted wires, knotted ropes,
sorrel, corrugated kale leaves—
none of the flowers
from the glossed book there that day—
just the shuttered-down, closed-off,
bleached emptiness; the winter
of the place . . .

where we started out,
stunted debris, Donne's unanswered rhetoric,
the horizon too near, the thunder imminent,
the two of us skimming stones,
a flat sea longing to be lit.

First Naming

In the calling mellow notes of the first bird
    Eve heard love, softness, open air, saw her own white body.
Dove! she said. *Bringer of peace.* Jubilant, the bird
    opened its throat wider, raised wings soared into the bright sky
triumphant. Suddenly Eve, too, felt free.
    How easy that had been.

But at the dark, glossy feathers of the next bird
    Eve paused, alive with other desires: ones she could not name,
black as the night sky, held tight inside like a fist.
    The dark bird hovered, craving its name.
Belying terror, Eve casually opened her hand—
    the fist inside—cried, *Raven!*

Eden

I've gone back to the place
where thought begins:
the rhubarb patch, white blossom,
a child's green swing

swaying. Something intangible is there,
a first word perhaps
like a seed, tooth-caught
then freed, to be negated

by other words. Ones that name
the garden of plenitude:
soil, sun, nettle, dock-leaf,
feather, dandelion, buttercup

and profligate Queen Ann's lace.
But a word or thing slips
subtly, between pine-cones,
chestnuts, the fruit red

for harvesting: darker than unease,
or blood, further back than memory—
belly slithers to a bough,
fang-sharp settles in the apple tree.

Postcard to my Brother
for Mike

Hotter than England, I scrawl on this postcard
a local scene (not one that makes me think of you)
to send to America where you live now: a house—stark,
white—squats against sea and sky in photographic blue.

Nearby an old goat languishes on a frayed rope;
rolled nets jut from trees in hillside olive groves,
all sun-still. I hardly recall Preston Sands or you,
goose-pimpled in a towel, reading Sherlock Holmes,

nor us smacked hard by stampeding waves,
as wind lashes stinging spray and sand
into our foolhardy faces while the red flag flies.
I've forgotten childhood, holidays in England.

Then today, unexpectedly, the sun scarcely breaks
through cloud: the sea is a furrowed English grey,
wind drives the waves; salt pangs the air. Now
you're here. Not in America, nor all those years away.

The Quietest Hour

Sounds like clichés
lull us into a slumber of security
like the shutter bang on a hot afternoon
or your breath at siesta time—
an unconscious rhythm
of whispered tenderness.

And even in that quietest hour
an incipient breeze hisses
at sun-idled poplars,
a dog yelps on the heat's perimeter,
a motorbike thrums on the track
between us and the sea.

Then far away but seeming near,
a drowse of voices, shush of waves
and the cicada's insistent see-sawing
could be today or years ago
at other resorts, on other trips
blurring, or so we like to think,
all unspoken distances.

Here, a man who walked out alone,
the sky white hot dangerous,
split our sleep one sultry afternoon,
a single gunshot
for the scream of it.

Arkansas Spring
for my mother

Miles from home
I look out of a first floor room

to write of birds,
whippoorwill, blue jay, robin, cardinal

but am drawn instead by the home-grown pull
of other things: white blossom petals

translucent in sudden rain.
Or flaring yellow forsythia.

And I remember you, years ago,
kneeling at a lawn's edge,

a golden tentacle
in your hand—

from any garden we had left behind
to lessen the leaving and the distance—

and you planting there
spring's bright filament.

Mother,

our worlds collide
through the slip and glide of time:
I'll remember the steep hump of the orchard,
its sporadic trees, more wasteland than fruit,
corn stubble, spearmint, sun-burn
and a boy I knew, his shouts cool and long,
across the park's disappearing green,
an arc of pallid sky, moments before the light died.

You'll remember Dr Scott's surgery:
high-backed chairs, incurably hard, bandages,
sniffs, coughs, the anaesthesia of magazines
and the voice of the boy's father, *I'll pay anything . . .*
anything . . . heard by everyone in the waiting room
unrestrained by the implacable fact of a door.

Now we coincide when you remark,
all these years on, *Mr Wilkes lost his wife to cancer,*
a nice woman . . . and I recall you mopping my head
when I was ill, then one day cramming a suitcase
to leave and not return, and how their son,
that boy I liked, didn't cry, but bleached his hair,
ran off from school. And how summer light
still haunts and hollows the evening sky.

The Sabbath

Because yesterday the cold dulled our road
I was sure it would snow and I longed
for an infinity of flakes, so I could write
of that new white on bushes, trees,
slope of roofs, a brightness,
cleansing my whole life, like baptism—

and because today the sun is a hazed gold,
(there was no snow) its warmth
eases us into almost summer,
images come:
the garden in late June, a dove, its tail fanned,
passion flowers opening, you with a watering can . . .

and because it is actually still winter,
the earth dry, and you're here
sitting at the table with a coffee, writing
in my journal is awkward,
as I wonder about words—
how they alter perception
or do I mean imagination?
my thoughts adrift, until suddenly I believe
a word is intercessory, like a shaman,
a priest at prayer, not an essence;
so with black ink on a page
clean for transformation,
I shape a lettered sacrament—
                              water, sunlit air.

Sunday School

A child's picture:
Jesus in an English Garden.

His cloak, a celestial blue,
leads from hunched shoulders

to the scribbled lines
for the tormented darkness

of a darker sky. Blood as sweat
streams to heaven, red

as drowsing poppies
through a half-remembered dream.

All the doubt we have in truth
betrayed by the blown back black

of dawn, and the naïve faith
we've found in naming

scrawled with an uncertain hand:
lavender, geraniums, a lawn of unripe plums.

The Word

Once upon a time —

The Word

Not aromatic lily.   Not spectre dove.

Not angelic light.   Not scourged flesh.

The Word.

Not redemptive love.   Not white crucifixion.

Not deified blood.   Not bright raiment.

The Word.

In the beginning —

Nascent.   Guttural.   Incandescent.

Annunciation

Zachariah is visited by an angel who says,
though both he and his wife are old, they will have a child

— LUKE 1 (5–63)

Nine mute months
pass in disbelief.
Zachariah stares, nightly, at the sky—

ordinary portent of God. No aurora
borealis of angel, gold, tower of radiance,
harbinger of birth

or other glad tidings. Unlike that time
at the temple where he, prostrate skeptic
in priest's robes, insists:

But I am old . . . Amid light, wings,
prophecy, the angel speaks: *Behold*
thou shalt be dumb,
until that day these things shall be performed.

He has not uttered since. His hand
ineffable, articulates
the final swelling of her belly—
Elisabeth's time imminent—
until Zachariah

cradles, bloody moment born, a son.
Scrawls a name. Stammers. Cries out
to a starry wilderness—

the stars echo *John . . . John . . . John . . .*

Salome Holding the Head of Saint John the Baptist
Painting by Bernardo Luini 1520

You could not understand how time-bright the stars were.
        Or how a painting would one day depict the moment
        you would gag and turn your face away.

What did you know about men? About desire?
        Death? Anything? *You'll be rewarded for it.*
        Ask whatever you wish. And so you dance

to arouse a king. After, without a second's glance at him,
        you tongue the words. Unkissed lips
        request for your mother the prophet:

John the Baptist. Who has entered your dream.
        Abandoned, you caress his beard and slip
        your fingers lower to the vulnerability of skin.

Unyielding, still a girl, under a mother's sway,
        the quixotic pull of dance, ignition of the stars,
        you demand again that never dreamt-of-thing.

Now in the picture you turn your eyes away.
        There is no starlight here. Only a man's head.
        His blood drips like paint. In time, congeals.

Dead Fox

I don't know now where we'd gone
but everywhere cars parked
nose to tail, and the yellow light
from aluminium framed windows
in the fish-and-chip shop,
now closed, still shone.

All that metallic glint,
even the nearest tree—
a shellac sheen in streetlights,
where someone had driven on
leaving a fox,
urban though it was, blood
damp on the tarmac
to be pulped, *strikes me*
you said, *as obscene.*

But if I'm honest,—
while you dragged it
to the kerb's double yellow lines—
the starless sky, hardly black—
I didn't think about a fox
left dead by some motorist.

I merely stopped myself staring
at the red redness of its blood.

Arkansas in March

Here things are slow colours:

ponderous red a truck starts, stalls.
A cat slinks black, lovers are a blue

amble of jeans. Sun
dissolves into the day's yellow drowse.

Here an event
is someone seen on a sidewalk, his wood house as slumberous

green as coned fir trees. Above, a hawk is a recumbent
brown on its wing-spanned breeze.

In an indolence of afternoon
clouds crawl

like words on the tongue's indigenous southern drawl.
Colours yawn the movement of things,

light is languorous,
the rain grays down.

Something that Happened

The dog was dead. We had travelled
a long way in the huge black
of a shut-up truck. Through sun-smart,
dirt, empty plains and tree sift of air—
now I remember the tournament, your legs burnt,
sun cream tubes squeezed for the very last bit,
the dog under a deck chair. His ribs slow rise,
the drool from his jaws, his tongue panting pink.
Us parking the truck for a creek, an old tap,
or tank, something—anything for him to drink. Only
a dried-out ditch by the town's wood sign: *Calistoga
Springs*. And on the dashboard saliva streaks
scratched windows, a hot vinyl smell, stick of my hands,
the sun's black-metalled heat. Then afterwards,
pushing salad about on a plate, the diner's fans,
like a bad secret, going round and round and round.

Oxford, Again

Our lives,
I read once, are nothing more than a sketch—

inconsequential lines drawn down by gravity,
like the portrait in the Ashmolean:

Raphael's *Head of an Unknown Youth* etched
in fine black lines,

and the faintest white, or that scene
I still recall—

a hot summer night, you by college walls,
charcoal smudges

of upturned boats, and on the river
the scribbled gold of lamplight.

Hopper's Canvas

SUMMERTIME

I see her now
in the morning's dull light

which breaks sometime into brilliance
and know from the way she chooses

then throws clothes
wanton over bed and chairs

she's imagining a lover,
and from the way her hands

smooth along petticoat satin
camisole silk, his flawless skin.

Hopper's painted what her day brings:
a breeze's warm fingers parting window nets,

its billowed sighs, the gossamer linger of her dress on breast and thighs,
hard shade, vacant pavement, sun-brunt.

COUPLES

Concentrated in a finger
all the expectation of her wedding day—

Hopper, how well you've caught this woman:
her husband and the room

silent, but for the rustle
of a newspaper as the breeze—hot

in darkening sky—
disturbs it. Her husband's

buttoned up in suit and tie,
his jaws clamped

hard as the city heat.
I can't explain why her red dress—

its softly sculptured neck
and arms' bare length—

do not invite. Nor why
her perfume—once like hyacinths—

cloys and stifles. Has he forgotten—
though it shines

like damask in the light—
her hair's silky feel

between his fingers,
the first night he'd dared

to touch her anywhere?
Above this picture

someone's written: *Hopper—a romantic
though others rarely*

measure up to one's ideal. Here, their painted
predicament: evening sulks,

she flirts with piano keys
and, as he turns over *The New York Times,*

her finger slips
to a lower note—discordant.

ROOMS — SEA

An old woman cuts the stems
of drooping lilacs, crowds them in a lambent glass,

their drift of scent
an intimacy against her husband's death.

As in Hopper's painted room:
no one there, a door flung wide,

untrammelled sea, gape of light.

ARRIVING IN NEW YORK CITY

Paralysed on pressed hotel sheets she reads the letter
in her downcast hands. Somewhere else a timber house
by the beach slumbers vacant now. Winter in a seaside town.

Her suitcase crammed with longings', closed. She's removed
her hat, dress, the shoes she bought for breaking out.
Here, no stinging spray, salt stench on wood groynes, no gull cries,

sun-bleached stone nor the lapping of the shore.
The elevator pings, but no-one comes to the plush
untrodden mat outside. She scans the letter's cramped,

familiar scrawl, her name its only flourish—
written by the fountain pen she gave him once. And rhythmic
from her balcony traffic sounds—an errant echo of the sea.

HOUSE AT DUSK

It's how on a Spring evening the place just is:
some blinds half-drawn show the shadows
of an interior. Brooding trees bulk in black,
by the house where a woman's looking out
to glimpse a man and an ambulance. For a moment
I'm caught by the way things stop, start,
end then begin—blue gaps in the sky,
the sun's spiral between the deadened drum
of unexpected showers. Or how May's blaze
of yellow rape becomes the mind's chasm
as dark seeps through all the green sear of Spring
and the whole world turns to night and rain.

Swans

Thursday, we talked of swans
tucked or ruffled

on a slate grey lake
and how, between the seeing

and the writing on a page,
something seismic moves

below the surface,
like dark subterranean plates.

These were Heaney's swans
glimpsed along the Flaggy Shore

in County Clare, where wind and wings
buffeting the car

catching someone off guard,
could erupt the heart's fault line.

I thought of swans I'd seen once
high above tarmac, pylons,

endless motorway signs. I longed
to find the words

for these swans:
flight-strong, glittering

in the sun, frost-feathered,
flung out white

against a winter sky
their wings wild-water-wide.

Maltas Beach

Greece 2003

The blue blink of bubbles behind us as we swim
    lead you to remark:
        It isn't God at work
                the sea cleans itself.
Science says, there's no transcendent.

So cycling back to our apartment
                I'm observant of the ordinary:
gaps and shapes in olive groves,
              the sculptured, curving bones of goats,
      cow parsley verges,
a peasant woman in spectacles,
        whose morning is a doorway's sun,
                  and wooden stool.

And the road's a miasma of tarmac,
              drain-stenched heat,
where at the bend yellow arrows
          securely point a future way
              then filter out,
                  directionless.

I see this is how the world explains itself,
            no God as such,

just a white-domed shrine with silver icon, glowing flame,

      and an attempt to sanctify Coke or lemonade.

Or a car upturned, abandoned,
            one rusty door ajar, faithful for the owner
who's already gone,
     inexplicably,
        some other way.

At the hill I think of God
      as once they thought the world was flat:

            desirable, but out-moded now.

Though in the warm wind fluster of speeding down,

             know there's still mystery
in the sea's slow blue self-cleansing

          and the day's cardiogram of water, light.

Lilies

A painting by Rogier van der Weyden c.1445
The vase of lilies are also a symbol of purity.

How easy then to forget Elisabeth

and the painter's need to paint the flowers.

As if Mary hadn't visited.   Bringing with her lilies.

White.
        Immaculate.
                Tremulous.   Cleaved

In air.

                    Angel-like.

Breakfast on Saturday

One of our common conversations:
art and artifice. You've been reading Milosz.
I've copied out part of his preface—
the problem: how to express
the inexpressible sense of being?

I'm squeezing oranges, enjoying
the squelch of pips and pulp,
and I'm feeling a sullen sadness
that's nothing more than a monthly thing
as you offer the metaphor of stone—
the poet hews, sculpts, carves
poems as chiselled forms, one by one . . .

My mind slips to Athens, a hot afternoon,
you lying on a white sheet, the window ajar,
the sun on corners, concrete, aerials,
the infinite of a city; the gift, hardly discernible,
of singing . . . and all that's missing

not part of the chiselling but present:
myself, the one orange on the table
still untouched, my sense of something spiritual
in the music. Somewhere beneath that hotel room
incessant drilling, and on my back your silent hands,
articulate tenderness.

Why Words Might Not

Her father in those closed off days before hospital
talking to the roses

Even if the Big Questions are Hard to Answer

and words may not refer to a world
old habits persist. At home
we still like to be sure: as sure as Sundays
when the neighbours hose their cars,
that what we see and name,
like the bird tacking for worms
on a primrose bordered lawn is
a starling, in all its starlingness.

But whatever was falling and rising,
rising and falling above the pier
was something else. As if somewhere
beyond massed cloud and warm breeze,
an unknowable force (once called God)
pulled a magnet this way, that. Now awed
only by form and shape, shimmering specks
in singular thousands, drawn across sky
like iron filings, bewilder us.

The Failing Light

She remembers now the oil stove
more clearly than anything. That and the snow,

and the way the failing light
closed off the sky. But he had been there

and she had thought that day
she would marry him.

She swore she would remember
his raw smell, saltiness,

his white skin, the way he tried
to reassure her,

just as he had the first time
leaving his gold signet ring

by her side when he'd gone off
and slept with someone else.

Instead it's his leaping out of bed
she remembers, the shivering

in the hall when the phone rang,
to learn her niece was born,

the cold sheets on her return,
the bed's stretch of emptiness,

and on the ceiling,
grown large in the snowed-down-dark

the pattern of the oil stove—
its black intricate shadow

that might have been a rose.

Mary Magdalen's dream

and how night long she dreams a garden
and how long becomes the shadow
and how the shadow seems a helmet
and how the helmet is a skull of stone
and how the stone is heaved in place
and how in place of feet dust-darkened bone
and how at once the dust thickens
and how once awake she gasps for breath
and how she gasps to the market-square
and how he gasps for breath as she—
and how for him unbraids her hair
and how they upbraid her at the price
and how the perfume's price defrays her
          prescience of death

*

Autumn

Hundreds more sites patrolled for signs of bird flu in Britain.
— *The Guardian* OCTOBER 2006

I want to mark the return of summer
in October: the sun's gold

long on nasturtiums that curl stems
and nudge buds in high profusion;

how parsley, mint and sage
are still an eloquent August lush.

And I want to write of your pleasure
in red crab apples, the rose hips' gloss

against the sky's slow blue; of how
I'll hang washing, see the swirling

poise of chrysanthemums, though nearby
strawberries hang still mouth-moist.

I want the garden's late exuberance
to be some trick of time

against the ravages of frost
to keep distant the insistent

cold that cuts the bone
and stop the beating wings

of swan, teal, pigeon, geese—
and all the other birds we've loved.

Summer now would mean
I hadn't walked through

October dew, nor read the news
of darkening skies alive with winter flight.

Salthouse Church

Winter. The land lies low. Rain-sunk.
Clotted bushes splinter rosemary along a path,
to the flint church whose tower cried up
across the centuries to a God-embodied sky.

Inside our echoes rise to the ribbed roof,
hollowed out by high stone arches.
Underfoot, stone slabs are worn smooth.
A knapped light lights on vacant pews.

Once hundreds in a service, now the few
seeking solace, kneel on a hassock,
cry into a cold cavern, *Our Father*
who art in Heaven: faithful orphans in the dark.

We leave—rain chill on our faces,
hedgerows wind-bend to the sea.
Out on the salt marsh a single tree
claws the sky. The church—a carcass.

Nightingale

November—when you always write. Your poems
mark decay: leaves (inevitably); chill on my brow;
dust on your tongue. My students read Keats
but the *beechen green*, his nightingale's

full-throated ease, or even *the thicket, fruit-tree,*
and fast-fading violets are too far away
this sombre month to mourn,
any spring-soft sound, the brevity of things.

November—you plant bulbs in ceramic pots,
I remember how one summer at dusk
we stood transfixed by some bird's melodious song
unable to move or speak until the singing stopped.

Winter Afternoon in Hampden Park

A dull snow sky.
In a half-shuttered room
a woman irons sheets
with iron-to-white exactness.

She thinks of a another country
the scent on the veranda,
a glimpse of the one road out
the small wood bridge,
the sand-amber beach, and a man
 who thumped and thumped
an octopus on white rock
in sunlight, the sea as blue
as the irises on her apron.
Even at the slow coming down
of dark, such heat.

The iron thuds harder
as if it could melt the snow sky.
The horizon's a line of spindled trees.
She longs for stars: huge, violent.

The Anchor

An anchor was that day's bequest,
        a rust jut in the sand, tide-tugged
a thousand miles, too heavy to yank,
                we bent and eased it out,
                      propped it by a damp wood groyne,
then hand in hand along the beach imagined the anchor's
                      plummet to the depths: an iron weight
against the smack of storm.

You tied it high up to a pole and there, above my head
                suspended
                    as if strangely light,
Nietzsche's conundrum came to mind: lived only once,
                  our lives are weightless,
but each moment,
        will come back exactly as it was:
an eternal cycle of return.

So, will this moment too, go on?
        You always tying a knot of rope to a sharp, stark anchor
                high
                    now in a sea-blue sky.
Would such recurrence
            become our heaviest burden
                or our lives' essential ballast?

Take your first caress,
            the lightness of your hand, light
like summer waves
        across burning sand. Who would not burn the now

of then into tongued flames again,
though there is always
            the lash and fret of things too pain-scorched to repeat?
And how can we understand the sea's rising and receding
                        eroding always—everything?

So with its weight
            and earthbound thrust,
                        held in your hands then roped to the sky,
this sea-cross of rust bequeaths corrosion,
                        not a moment that will return—
                                    and also love.

Remembrance Sunday

In memory of Jenny
Cambridge 2007

We stand in the market for two minutes
to remember. Wind taunts the jaunty tatter
of stalls, scarves, coats, red-pinned poppies.
Leaves, Autumn's lightest medals, scatter.

And I think of last August, not the many deaths;
I was prepared for Italy, when your daughter rang,
then your husband, matter of fact: your breath,
at the end, came from merely half of half a lung,

how you'd gasped for something to focus on.
It's not the troops, air-raids, bombs, planes,
nor the Cenotaph's wreaths for those long gone,
I recall this November, but your death ingrained

in the Tiber's languorous summer ease,
in the sun-green stasis of silent trees.

Garra Rock

And the end and the beginning were always there
before the beginning and after the end.

T.S. Eliot

We must remember: *all is always now.*
So, today I'm at Garra Rock—the steep jag of descent,
us clambering down.

I hear your *Look! Look!* wind-slung to the horizon;
see the gannets' perfect plumb-line drop—
perpendicular flight programmed for their constant dive.

Generation after generation genes go on
repeating themselves: coded chromosomes,
nucleic acids, proteins, enzymes, ribosomes . . .

Here, now . . . always now: the boy paddling with his father.
And you, arms akimbo, remarking,
how alike they seem:

Same shoulder droop, squat stance, pallid flesh,
shortened arc from neck to head. Life to come
fixed a million years before any one life has begun.

Quick now, here—
Now, your son, only four then, cautious, skirting the water's edge.
You, cross-armed, longing to plunge like gannets headfirst in.

Generation after generation—
me, exultant (my parents taught me how to swim),
leaping in the toss and drag of that day's sea-wind convulsion.

Generation after generation genes go on
repeating themselves. Coded chromosomes,
Nucleic acids, proteins, enzymes, ribosomes
go on . . .

And can you see the frenzy—
drenched towels,
a soaked sandal,

your book being flung,
when an errant tidal tongue, as it has always done,
hurls the blueprint of the future in?

Though that day years ago has gone,
The salt stain on our lives then
Here, now, quick—immediate.

Held

Not by nails hard into wood.

Not as a vinegar sponge souring lips.

Not in memories we don't have, but those we imagine we do:

shadow shrouding a cool room, a window's small light,
unrisen bread, a simple pitcher, red stain of spilt wine:
blood through a cloth's white,
                              and you remarking,
                                        casually,
                    you'd come back for good.

Kispum
Syrian memorial ritual

It's the stillness in the morning,
the way the blind ticks slow

against the open window
as the sun breaks gold

after days of slab-grey cloud
and that *National Geographic*:

an owl believed extinct, now found,
(its yellow stare penetrating

through the whirl of snow
and blizzard temperatures

unimaginably cold) makes me think
we know ourselves in something lost

and then retrieved: an old love letter,
the photograph of a grandmother

I never met, last year's diary,
leather bound, your arms around me

after our fiercest row. And how in the mind's
fan-feathered flight, its black shadow

an oblivion on the ground.
I turn the pages of the magazine

to an excavation of a sealed tomb
where once the living went

to feast and be blessed
by the buried bones of kings.

Conundrum

That we know ourselves by what we say and feel is obvious.
Or in the way we lay a table, chop an apple, hang clothes or not,
                                        before we sleep.
And it's obvious, too, that such knowledge must include:
the birthmark on an inner thigh, mouse-shaped, small;
a jagged lifeline on a left hand; finger-prints, the iris pattern of an eye.
Or in the way one scuffed shoe slants to nothing at the heel;
and in the exact marks of our feet before waves slur the sand.

These are ways we seem fixed. But what about the self
                                        in a photograph?
The one we look at, intermittently, across our lives:
a shy child in a new pair of dungarees, now faded;
not looking at the camera, or a life ahead;
someone we would never recognise as us,
though that's precisely who it is.
And who is it that always leaves a drawer half-opened,
tilting down to show off what's inside:
a matted brush, blunt scissors, rusted key,
to tell about another self—someone, today,
                                we can't remember ever was?

And who is it looks in mirrors over years?
Like the familiar person in a dream—the one you cannot name—
who does the things you would, and who, like you, shuffles by the sea,
stares back, smiles all the same. Then slips effortlessly,
into, not obviously, a stranger,
                                but simply someone else.

Carrion

Last night the peaked cap you always wore
    back to front was in my dream
                and your eyes hungry, naively bold,
as they must have been, until
                a father at seventeen.

When we met, your sleeves were tied with string
                against the cold
and any place warm,
    like the barn you slept in, welcoming.

And you told me once
                how you'd scraped a young rabbit off the road
skinned, made a fire, eaten the whole thing.

By then you had a restless look-
                hawking stuff at jumble sales,
rummaging in dustbins
    raking every roadside skip
                ravenous for everything.

But we all have other selves,
                and married now
        on holidays you send picture postcards from Bali:
of girls,
        bare-limbed, shy-glanced,
                beckoning;
        write of a rich Japanese wife as blossom in the spring.

Waking out of sleep, I understand why you married her—
                wonder about the you,
    half-starved, scavenging rabbit,
                vulva red with dark pubescent fur.

The Hour of the Wolf

The hour between night and dawn, when most people die,
when sleep is the deepest, when nightmares are most real . . .

— INGMAR BERGMAN

Sleepless 5am.
I'm looking at a postcard.
Trees, lamp posts,
black and sentinel, stare back
as the river's mist
creeps into the threat of distances.

I look and shiver in this almost dawn,
What draws me to this picture?
The two faceless figures
who will never turn round, their unforgiving backs?
Dreamlike, they will always be unknown,
caught with ghostly blurs of breath on hard-frost ground.

One man stands motionless
(though there's a swell to the wind)
as if he's caught, suddenly,
slower, smaller, hunched against the cold,
an older self, who shuffles on ahead.

What obsesses us about a place
real or imagined,
is a memory, dream, or what we sense
will come. In this November hour
as you still sleep
I stare again at the wall, the river,
Autumn's thinning out of trees.

What haunts me in this postcard:
light
that startles as it brightens
beyond the cut of shadows,
the scatter fall of leaves.

Cobwebs

A wish for words that adhere to who we really are.
              — MILOSZ

In their flimsy connectives
           sunlit silks
                        a faint or ancient
   longing
of what we want to say
               should language ever free us.

You gave me honeysuckle,
              pale gold petals so open now—
their stamens, interior antennae,
                 of backyard silences:

paths with sage, parsley, mint;
      nasturtium trails,
          ivy tendrils dark, memorial
            and you climbing a thin ladder for the
     honeysuckle,
shimmered leylines
          from the heart.

Between Things

A word for the moment when a crow
caw seems black night, although light

lightens the window blind; when sheep huddle
down dark and diamante mist rises

or when enamelled yellow
buttercups in shade are still sun mirrors

and the prospect of change is wind
oscillating poplar leaves.

A word, too, for when the mind meanders
And—as if on air—memories come, flit, land precise

on random things:
black barred gates, a sun-cloud sky,

my mother her coat and hair damp—
drizzle diaphanous as insect wings.

The Words to Say It

I.

I read today in a poem
about moonlight
on bed covers and tangled sheets

Image of delight
Or longing
Or torment

Depending on who's
Doing the imagining.

I liked the openness of this,
until I found your postcard:

a French village, early evening,
the sun mellow on the rocks
and on the bricks of the houses
at the quay's end.
                    The light
made everything in the water
shimmer possibility.

You sent it from Addenbrookes,
Cambridge. You were having chemo,
you were the one who was *doing* . . .
the verb you used on the card: *pretend.*

II.

Sometimes there's only euphemism.

III.

Christmas Eve, my partner and I stopped
at Birling Gap, the wind surprised us (where,
in mid-summer heat, a girl ran naked
across the rocks into the sea,
her skin opalescent in the sun).

Now I recall the lights:
amber spots on the pub's three-rose award,
the tinsel hung in loops across the windows
glittering, and driving up to Beachy Head
(the trees, horizontal claws, as if make believe
from a child's picture book)
there was the long-poled beam
from the Chaplain's jeep
back and forth, random and mad
like a—like a—but no likenesses come,
only that dark search
interrogating the cliff
shocking me from speech.

Like—your daughter's voice in August:
Sunday, Mum passed away.

IV.

The thesaurus offers a list: *dying, end,*
ruin, symbols of . . . transience.

v.

Branches of trees hang black
and thin as wet hair in the mist.
The owl box newly made
by the man (whose teenage son, last year . . .)
is in the hall, too heavy to lift.

My almost granddaughter
wants the tulip tree we've bought
to remember you,
planted next to hers: the one
to celebrate her name, her birth.

Where is your friend now? she asks.

In my mind the displacing power of art:
the undiscovered country . . .
no traveller returns . . .

and words like *heaven, spirit . . . not on earth*

your cancer; and us, standing there wet with mist
by the tennis court (far–off laughter and the August
twang of a ball on a net), the clarity
in this small girl's eyes, her red hat . . .

VI.

In the thick dark of a Norfolk night
my headlights' beam once
on a barn owl, low flying, haloed.
Ahead, it seemed for hours, beckoning,
                    white as imagined snow . . .

                              and then
the bird, or the image, or the words
were gone as lightly as feathers,
as slowly as breath, some place else.

VII.

Unsayable.

VIII.

It's the mind's art
to make the past seem present for us:

white blossom in January—almost sky
until you really look. Blossom—a symbol?
You're in that auburn wig,
which suited and depleted you,
made you someone else, and more yourself—
or so friends said—bringing out
the colour of your eyes.

IX.

You used capital letters
on the postcard:

COME SOONEST.

The whole sentence read:
*I'm pretending I'm in France —
not Addenbrookes.*

We write these things because
we are what we imagine:

wings and flowers
—tulips were your favourite—
an owl's dark flight, a child running,
sheets, bedclothes, Beachy Head,

the flexing of a searchlight . . .

My Father's Tin Box
for my father

Every paper that mattered to you,
you filed there, in its rectangular, fire proof,
indestructible cabinet grey.
A reliquary for your life: out of date
insurance numbers, mortgages, bills,
birth certificates, even my school reports
creased with age, and your will—
This box, an archaeologist's find,
with sprung lock that, unfailingly,
snaps shut or flips up may come to me
when you die . . .

On my way to Santorini this summer
I imagined your tin box—
after a massive earthquake
like the one when the Minoans
were wiped out—as a metal amphora,
strangely buoyant, burning mysteriously,
as if magnesium on the water: a calm
survivor, untouched by the magma's
catastrophic eruption of steam and lava;
and me, your middle daughter,
in that black Aegean cataclysm.

The Fruit of Poetry
for Andrea and Todd

How easy to forget, as you open
a tin of peaches in Arkansas,
the soft fur skin of a fresh peach—
yellow or pink even bruised maybe,
with a darker reddish blush on one side,
or forget the squelch of juice, flesh,
threads that cling to stone and teeth.

How easy too, reading poems
about hard times, to forget the rest,
except that in your careful placing
of the peach bowl,
I see my mother, years ago,
on our settee in her dressing gown,
(not having dressed all day), calling
there's a tin of peaches in the cupboard
open them if you like . . .
Her way to offer a treat
on an English Sunday afternoon.

I hated the cupboard stacked
with all kinds of tins
just in case we ran out of money
or maybe even love.
But I still ate the smooth peaches
slippery in their sweet syrup glisten
and fresh peach then, a luxury
I simply hadn't had.

Now I eat with relish
what I know now
is the same taste the world over—
peach from a tin,

but wish at each mouthful
time was a treat
to be opened up, poured out,
served unexpectedly to sustain.

Postcard of a Swan

whose sculptured wings of white intent
and powered feet detonate

a thousand incandescences as it lands
on a river somewhere I'm imagining

but haven't seen: the Tigris or Euphrates.
I think of ancient civilisation,

my school history book, a physics lesson
on how the earth was formed,

the trip (years ago) to the Planetarium
and peering up in the domed dark

at an immutable moon and stars,
their stark illumination.

Yesterday I read a page on relativity,
about how the earth began

with a few red wisps, ashes, smoke,
a dense finale of the bang and hurl

of matter and how the universe
is infinite, webbed

and continues to expand.
Though now I'm caught

by intimacy: the curvature of light
on a swan's wing, the way days speed

or slow. And how, near or far,
on another space—time continuum,

Einstein's wife mentions to a friend
in the kitchen, one rainy day,

he wrote E=MC² at home
on the back of an envelope.

The Necessity of Judas

In that sparse garden,
his lips press on Christ's cheek

the pressure
of accomplishment.

Where We Begin

for my sister

may be a concealed paradise
           with the radiance of words married to a world

lit by memories and presence:
           friends, family, failing
falling stars, nuclear power,
      that sprig of rosemary you've just picked, aromatic, in your palm,
fairy tales, betrayal in Gethsemane, long horizons, ravens,
           candy floss, the spat-out sharp of plums.

           Where sometimes I imagine angels,
Magdalen's slow-soothing perfume,
           her unbraided hair, and in our yearning
for sanctity and sacrilege:
           the homeless self we have become.

But on this hot evening in July,
           it's simply our backyard, jasmine
confettied on a path,
           the scent of mint *redemptive*.

The Words for Home

Not the place I thought
where there are clichés

for nightfall or where hillsides
from the bathroom window

are the silver nouns
for an olive grove. Nor our flat

and the midnight street
we look out on

under the moon, its neon
and litterblown shouts

or echoes of catcalls
from the train track

where the act of naming
is *Tesco's or Ladbrokes.*

But somewhere
in the grammar

of the senses —
whispered imaginings:

a dust road to the coast
with blue waves

and rock that glitters
like glass,

where we swam
in the semantics

of salt-water, sunlight.
The wind stirring the pampas.

Summer afternoon at the Cuckmere

We drove through mist, familiar landmarks
sudden hunched spectres, silent, indistinct
looming from the cling of damp. The pool
where we stopped—choked weed, stagnant.

In the clam of afternoon a single iridescence,
a fly, buzzingly alive. You pointed out a cow
lying down. *Expecting rain*, I thought, till I saw
a large lump, black and bloody like a lethal bruise.

A stillbirth. I could just make out in the air's thick:
two tangled calves, the cow's rear open,
raw from the expulsion of its knotted cargo.
The cow dead too. Then an ear flicked,
and with magnificence she strained,
heaved up her head. For a second it rose—
to thump back down on sodden ground.

Five brown bullocks lumbered up.
their blunt heads bent. They licked the dead,
nuzzled them, moved slowly on,
phantoms in the mist. The only sound
their listless rasping over grass.

Miles from Litlington

I hate this: the way the car seat sticks and clams
as we drive in pressing traffic

around a roundabout again,
as if our turning's lost and can never be retrieved.

It's four in the afternoon; girls in open white blouses
saunter down streets

careless of home or school,
aware only of their bodies' hot, languid lilt

to adulthood. A copper mist before the storm at Pevensey,
sorrel's rust, blue dragonflies,

an old barn's shadowed slats
and the Hopper house lined by light

magnify these recent days.
We stop the car on an unfamiliar road,

stare, as if through glass,
at a cornfield,

each grained yellow ear of corn motionless,
for mile upon mile, precise, sunlit.